ANCHOR BOOKS

RHYME IN REFLECTION

Edited by

Steve Twelvetree

Dear Gill & Eric.
So many loving
words enclosed
Trust it helps a
little

First published in Great Britain in 2000 by
ANCHOR BOOKS
Remus House,
Coltsfoot Drive,
Woodston,
Peterborough, PE2 9JX
Telephone (01733) 898102

All Rights Reserved

Copyright Contributors 2000

HB ISBN 1 85930 832 5
SB ISBN 1 85930 837 6

Lots of Love.
FOREVER YOUR
Friend.
Stella Page
xxx 79.
Feb. 4TH 2001.

FOREWORD

Rhyme In Reflection invites you to enjoy the simple art of rhyming verse.

From the moment when poetry took the hand of a more modern and complex style, the traditional form of rhyming poetry seems to have taken a back seat.

In this truly magnificent collection of rhyme, the fun has been brought back with energy and ease.

Both easy to understand and relate to, these poets have allowed us to share their lives and intimate thoughts.

The reader is sure to gain an insight into the hearts and minds of these traditional poets.

Be inspired by this purest form of poetry, it's sure to be a winner in the eyes of many a rhyming poet.

Steve Twelvetree
Editor

CONTENTS

INDIAN SUMMER

'I'm not ready to go yet,' said Autumn,
tossing her tawny hair -
so that flurries of tiny fire-gold leaves
threw colour everywhere.

'I'm much too young to retire,' laughed Autumn,
tying her crimson shawl:
then she picked the diamonds that dew had hung
on cobwebs by the wall.

'How can I move just now?' argued Autumn,
'There's still much to be done.'
The warmth of her smile made berries ripe and
chestnuts gleam in the sun.

'Don't try to rush me,' pleaded shy Autumn,
painting her face with care,
till her blushes spread in the sunset and
made magic in the air.

'Please don't spoil my flowers,' whispered Autumn,
one cold and misty day;
but she shivered as tears from scudding clouds
washed their colour away.

'Why can't you leave me alone?' pouted Autumn,
as bonfire smoke curled high:
then, defiantly, as a farewell fling
hurled fireworks at the sky.

Pat McDonald

HUSBAND

From the moment I saw those leonine eyes
I knew I was destined to be
Under your spell and you under my skin
Forever to be you and me

I still cannot explain how it felt
That I'd known you all of my life
Like two souls reunited
We were destined to be husband and wife

From the moment we touched the connection was true
All secrets held dear to impart
To trust one another with each other's worlds
No fear of a risk to the heart

Together against the tide of doubt
The timing for others was wrong
But we knew then and now they all see
To each other we will always belong

Together we can face anything
All the bad luck we seem to go through
It could be life's counterbalance
To the day that I met you

If I was asked what I would wish
For the world let alone all of my friends
It would be that they all find the happiness I have with you
And that like mine it would never end

Karen Naylor

THE RIVER SPEAKS

The river speaks of times gone by
In thunder rushing down from high.
She tells a tale so deep and wide
Of power held within the Clyde,
Harnessed and used in mills nearby

Making cotton then onto dye
In colours pleasing to the eye.
At New Lanark, mill of Strathclyde,
                    The river speaks.

Man, woman, child working each try
To make a living, not to die,
So each in their work takes great pride
With cloth to weave and shuttle to guide.
Amid the sounds that amplify,
                    The river speaks.

Annie McLean

ENDEAVOUR

My soul has soared to heights surpassed by none,
yet still I stand alone midst thoughts of you;
the joy we found still warms like noonday sun,
your tender touch so soft . . . long overdue.

So many miles between our lips does find
me caught 'twixt timid doubt that does condemn
the need for sanity and peace of mind
to hold each precious moment by its stem.

'Tis madness that we cannot be as one,
yet still I live in hope, with fierce belief
that someday, when we will our fears outrun,
surrender to our needs with sweet relief.

One truth alone stands brave to verify;
of creeping common-sense I shall not die.

Linda Zulaica

HEART AND SOUL

It is not in my nature to complain,
but honestly sometimes I feel so sad,
and I find it so hard to hide my pain,
although I don't regret the life I've had.

I hope and pray that before I pass on,
that God will smile down and bless me anew,
I wonder where my soulmate, she has gone -
ignoring my love which is pure and true.

My expectations are simple, easy to fulfil,
someone to share this life given by God,
but once more alone I find myself, still,
one set of footprints where once I trod.

It is not in my nature to complain,
I just can't face my loneliness again.

Bill Hayles

THE JOYRIDER

As midnight approaches, the excitement arises
Darkness has fallen, silent, dark, lonely nights.
I feel the adrenalin build up inside,
I need a car to get me through the night.
As I close my eyes, try to relax,
Images of fast cars dance in my head,
sports cars, police cars, BMWs,
the faster the better, so long as I'm driving.
I can hold back no longer, the obsession is thriving
and off I go into the dark of the night.

It may be borrowed, lent or stolen, but it gives me a thrill
and that's all that counts.
Accelerating, stalling, people calling,
reversing, skidding, then running, falling.
And as quick as a flash, it all ends.
Silence, emptiness and the cold eerieness of the dead
is all that remains
and nothing will ever be the same,
the game is up.

Locked wards, prison corridors, gloomy days lay ahead,
grown men sobbing, screaming, shouting.
Innocent people now lay dead.
Darkness, depression, dreary days,
were now all he ever knew
and he had had enough.
He cried for his mommy, his daddy too,
he cried through the night for the life he once knew.
For he was too young for a life like this
and wondered if he would ever be missed.

The prison rules were harsh and strict
and now he was to learn the harsh lessons of reality.
His mom, his dad, the victims too,
all say he left this world too soon.
So many wasted lives, so many days unspent,
such sadness and such waste,
to find him slaughtered in his bed.

S Akerman

MY INNER SELF

I wake up, my day has begun,
My spirits are lifted, my hopes are high,
I lay in my bed and look at the sun,
I must get up and I do with a sigh.

Why do I feel this way?
I don't have the answer.
It is such a wonderful day,
But inside I feel like a monster.

I have a lot of things to do today,
Papers to read, people to see.
I wish I could just get away,
Go to a place just to be free.

I go for a walk to clear my mind,
The clouds are gone, I feel like singing.
My heart feels glad, now that I am found,
I feel better now but this is just the beginning.

Suzann J Taylor

THAT LOVELY DAY

That lovely day, so long ago,
But still remembered well, you know.
We were so young; and people said,
'How silly to be getting wed,
You're heading for a life of woe!'

'Not true. We love each other.' So,
We proved the cynics wrong. And lo!
This year we celebrate instead
That lovely day.

When leaves of autumn gently blow,
Foretelling of the winter's snow.
The twilight years we shall not dread
On happy mem'ries we'll be fed;
Recalling in a golden glow,
That lovely day.

Phyllis Spooner

GLORIOUS MOMENTS OF LOVE DIVINE

Wantonness will be always at bay
If you live the Godly way
Showering love as you walk along
Talking to everyone with a willing tongue
'Please do have a happy day.'

Doing good is no doubt here to stay
You will feel happy and gay
Walking with a merry throng
Glorious moments of love divine

Free as a mischievous jay
Eating fruit yet, nothing to pay
Squawking with a voice like a gong
Yet, happy be he with his chirping song
We still admire him come what may
Glorious moments of love divine.

Alma Montgomery Frank

I KNEW

I knew then that you were different,
But for us this path was never meant.
I thought that you could make me whole,
Give heaven's wings to my wounded soul,
A joy that I could not relent.

You were the one that fate had sent,
The angel that the Lord had lent.
But I heard the bell begin to toll,
I knew it then.

I knew inside your lust was spent,
Watched blackened clouds in their descent,
Knew friendship would assume love's role.
Watched as mounting seconds stole,
Those feelings that were prominent.
I knew it then.

Danielle Morey

THE WAY IT WAS

The way it was before that May,
and we both threw our lives away,
this could not be created in a dream,
who could have thought that everything
was not as it might seem,
how could it all end in such disarray?

We followed our emotions and let them
have their sway,
I never had devotion shown in that
particular way,
surely this cat had now got the cream,
the way it was before that May.

But, like a bee who's sucked the pollen
dry, you had to stray,
did you have to do this thing until my
hair turned grey?
Or, was I just a kitten on the couch of
your harem?
Though I was not a painter, I could do
that silent scream,
it would be impossible to get it back
you'd say,
the way it was before that May.

Jean Paisley

TEMPTATION

Temptation surrounds whatever one's age,
Across a room eyes offer invitation
For dazzling flirtatious assignation,
Pressure increasing, hypnotising to engage,
She flattered, flicks lashes to disengage,
Glances again drawn by gravitation,
His dynamic look fires imagination,
Urging her open new romantic page.

She pauses, her marriage has survived dull years,
Gambling would risk losing her loyal loved one,
A dalliance will only end in tears
And a guilt handicap never outrun,
Let ladykiller pass, he will disappear
To green field pastures for sporting fun.

Hilary Jill Robson

A GIFT OF COMPLIANCE

Today you chose a bunch of red roses
Their colour added joy to these drab lives
In glimpsing Heaven how the spirit thrives
As we follow the dictates of noses.
Yours is sensitive to this piquant smell
With a trace of pollen we hear you sneeze
As its potency issues new decrees
That we like babes shall play at kiss and tell.

Ah! But are we too old for those cute tricks?
Second childhood seemingly disagrees
As cameras click and someone cries 'Cheese.'
A neighbourly idea - sharing the kicks.
Do generous gestures induce a song
With music muted that hearts may belong?

Patricia Howe

THE PLANKING'S GONE

The world is not yours and mine anymore,
it never was but you get the idea,
Like a beached whale breathing its last on shore,
I'm marooned at the end of the pier.

Beyond stretches waves of computerized thought,
net surfers speed by me com. dottily,
Primed by the gamblers for cyberspace sport,
I'd hoped, in my heart, they'd forgotten me.

Compassionless human technology,
viral infection prone, as everyone,
Zombie-like lumbering, ominously,
and retreat is not on . . . the planking's gone.

Electronics do all but defecate,
and long for that we should not have to wait.

Frank Valentine

BEHOLD!

Kind Muse you are more erudite than I,
Show me your love, a green isle in the sea,
Like furnaces let Bardic lovers sigh
And bring a new sprung red red rose to me.
They say you are half angel and half bird,
O lyric love, a fountain and a shrine,
Yet you are blind, a thing apart I've heard,
A choking gall when two young hearts entwine,
A madness most discreet to be reviled,
For 'all she loves is love' Lord Byron found,
And 'each man kills the thing he loves' said Wilde,
How can such passion make the world go round?
    But then I turned my head and caught your eye,
    And blessed my Muse as love came laughing by.

Peter Davies

A TIME FOR LOVE

There is a time, it's said, when love strikes home,
When nothing else distracts the mind, though skies
Fall, winds rage, injustice prevails and roam
In life's passing dire, crippling, haunting lies.

Love transforms, love gilds, love blinds, love rigs
The scales with which we weigh ourselves, each word,
Each action and intent. Love uses wigs,
Costume, make-up to make all be absurd -

Except for the sight, the breath, the feeling
And the tremulous happiness that flows
From the knowledge that you and I - reeling -
Have discovered that rich world that allows

Freedom to be all that ever was or
Will be to one another - and yet more!

S V Batten

No Microphone

The notes ascended like skylarks in flight,
as swift as prayers we offer the Lord;
humbled we listened, revering their might,
rocketing rightly the heavens toward.

A vision, a vessel of works of art,
the girl whose sweet carolling soared above,
urgent plea from the soul, honey from heart,
interpreting youth's rich version of love.

The sound craved neither enhancement nor aid,
like a comet aspiring into space,
artless, to music's climax unafraid,
such moment making a shrine of one place,

when everything near need come to a halt,
proof of nirvana, the gods to exalt.

Ruth Daviat

Times Of Old

There is a place I love to go
Where dwells the ancient full of wisdom
There to feast upon stories of old
Quietly stealing away depression, anxiety abandoned
To watch the kettle boil upon the peat
Fragrance filling the smoky air
Solemnly to behold sockless feet
The staff of life is scarce indeed.

Little amusement except for stories told
The night seems long and dark
No painted nails or glamour to behold
Faces aglow with firelight or forward spark.

Through flickering glow of candlelight beholding the past
There through the gloomy stillness shadow is cast.

Frances Gibson

WHAT DID WE KNOW OF WAR?

What did we know of war?
Just children, still at play,
What was it all for?

If there was a life before,
It changed, from that first day,
What did we know of war?

Loved ones, gone for evermore,
Childhood hadn't time to stay,
What was it all for?

Enemy bombers' throbbing roar,
Flames, turning night to day,
What did we know of war?

Anguished tears, behind closed door,
What was there left to say?
What was it all for?

Mindful of things we saw,
Memories, that ever stay,
What did we know of war?
What was it all for?

Evelyn Mary Eagle

RIVER'S LAW

Slowly the river drifts past,
Ripples along the surface plain:
Now again smooth as glass.

Little water in the river,
Soon will be high again;
Slowly the river drifts past.

Sun reflects the willows,
Weeping though with little rain.
Now again smooth as glass.

Fish under shady banks,
Frogs jumping once again.
Slowly the river drifts past.

Soon the river will flood again,
Weirs will roar some frightening game.
Now again, smooth as glass.

Cattle in the river middle;
Thirst for water and rain.
Slowly the river drifts past,
Now again smooth as glass.

Pamela Hopes

DEEPLY IN LOVE

Enjoy having you close to me,
When I take you out, can't go Dutch,
Deeply in love as I can be.

Our fun I want others to see,
I laugh while you I gently touch,
Enjoy having you close to me.

With you around I feel so free,
When separated it hurts much,
Deeply in love as I can be.

Know from you I will never flee,
Because we can't argue as such,
Enjoy having you close to me.

I have known you since you were three,
In my arms, I want you to clutch,
Deeply in love as I can be.

Want you to be with me, I thee,
Now bunny go back to your hutch,
Enjoy having you close to me,
Deeply in love as I can be.

S Mullinger

I Feel Like I Am Goin' To Die

I feel like I am goin' to die.
Life will be aimless without you
Now that you call to say goodbye.

I beg you, can't you tell me why
You're leaving without more ado?
I feel like I am goin' to die.

Love used to be in ev'ry sigh.
Will happiness really be through
Now that you call to say goodbye?

There was that moment when the sky
Saw dreams of you and me come true . . .
I feel like I am goin' to die.

And, worst of all, you don't deny!
So is there nothing I can do
Now that you call to say goodbye?

Must be a nightmare, passing by
Cloaked in horrendous moody blue! . . .
I feel like I am goin' to die
Now that you call to say goodbye.

Mike Roysons

DOOR OF FORGIVENESS (CELL 490)

A grudge did I dream in envenomed mind,
My Lord to His house did beckon me then,
Instead of a room a cell was assigned
Which numbered four hundred fourscore and ten.

Pondering hard how to have myself freed,
His voice did hear with remorse 'Don't you know?
Search out the number of times we agreed
To trespass forgive and love then bestow.'

The Lord with compassion did fast review
This door so locked by incongruity,
'Forgive and requite who sin against you,
Acknowledge them all, herein lies the key.'

Seven times seventy turned it thus far,
Leaving the door of forgiveness ajar . . .

A sonnet in forgiveness.

Roger Mosedale

LADY OF THE NIGHT

Oh come ye lovely ladies of the night
Who ply your trade away from people's sight
In winter's winds and under starry skies
Who cares for you or hears your piteous cries
Shunned by the righteous who do not understand
This never was the life that you had planned
But kids need feeding and shoes on their feet
So nightly you walk this ungodly beat
By what chance did this all happen to you
Don't say you don't know or haven't a clue
Because you had the choice. You chose the view
Don't make excuses or blame another
You made the choice. You chose the lover
Ended with four kids. You are the mother.

June Clare

THE EMERALD RIDERS

For Mary Marley fancy free,
Two suitors cross the Irish Sea,
She loved them both at the same time,
Paddy O'Neale and John Devine.

Rode handsome horses came in haste,
She'd wed the winner, let them race.
Paddy's mare as black as coal,
Stole from the fairies when a foal.

Flirty Mary, bow she had,
Promised to Dan, the stable lad.
He watched the Irishmen in rage,
Neither will have his pretty maid.

Saddled his master's stallion Swift,
He'd stop them when they topped the cliff.
Drummed the thunder of their hooves,
Shook the slates upon the rooves.

All cheered the rivals racing by,
Disturbed, the hounds set up a cry.
First neck and neck, then leads the mare,
Her flashing legs outpace the hare.

John, his chestnut frantic spur,
Slash his whip without a care.
Again, now neck and neck they fight,
Atop the cliff both rear with fright.

Hides Dan concealed within a bush,
A scarecrow on a pole he push.
Both horses leap away and shy,
Over the cliff, with deathly cry.

Smashed on the razor rocks below,
Spinning, the Irish suitors go.
Food to glut the greedy gulls,
Go picking in their bloody skulls.

The boiling sun he dries their bones,
Black Cross, the door, their Emerald Homes.
'pon England's cliff, ghosts to become,
And Dan the stable lad was hung.

A E Doney

THE KNIGHT

He was a knight from long ago
But no one knew his name
He always came to the rescue
Of a damsel who was to be slain

He would ride up to them
To release them from their doom
And they wanted to reward him
By making love to him in their room

The knight was very modest
To be wanted in this way
He would always decline their advances
They happened every day

The damsels were all smitten
By the armour that he wore
All they could see was his eyes
They wanted him more and more

Now the damsels gathered together
And planned to have their wicked way
They wanted to have the knight
In his uniform of that day

He was a hero to them
An icon in their eyes
The damsels hatched a plan
To trap him by surprise

Now on this particular day
The knight was riding by
When he did suddenly hear
A damsel's roaring cry

As he approached the damsel
Their plan it was all set
As he was about to free her
Down dropped a giant net

Finally they had him in their clutches
But they soon found out something was wrong
When they tried to take off all his armour
They discovered it was all welded on.

Niall McManus

IMMORTAL SOULS

Oh young love such ecstasy lost in time
Our hearts entwine oh such love most divine
Forget me not my love I cannot live
My soul it does not rest I cannot give

I am but a shadow lost in darkness
I feel our bodies embrace there is no pain
So fair my love beauty beyond compare
I'm but a cloud of dust that lies in sleep
I am immortal such love we will keep

Oh my heart I cry slumber deep in peace
We shall meet one day my love I will pray
I shall come to you like a burning light
We shall be as one like a bird's sweet song

MKF Dunn

THE BALLAD OF THE JOURNEY

She travelled to a foreign land
From a land of ice and snow.
Cold and barren stretched the hills,
The croft was long and low.
The animals moved steadily
Within the walls of stone,
And from that godforsaken place
She travelled far alone.
She moved across bare country.
She moved across the sea.
She kept on travelling steadily
Until she came to me.
She came to where I laboured.
She looked me thro' and thro'.
Without a word she cast her coat
And laboured with me too.
We laboured on throughout the life
Until one day she'd gone,
And oh, so much I miss her,
For now I am alone.

Pettr Manson-Herrod

THE AVENUE

As I walk down the avenue
narrow cobbled road, no grassy view.
Back-to-back houses, small and bleak
rented, in poor repair, our health defeats.

Wooden lathe, plaster and hair walls
riddled with vermin, bug-ridden as a result.
This was home for eleven years
caused sickness in children, misery and tears.

Diphtheria, whooping cough, bronchitis severe
coal-fired, smog atmospheres, could not be cleared.
All added to the fight to keep clean
contributing to the post-war misery.

Outside privy, copper with stack
was lit for hot water, the grime to attack.
Clothes washed by hand, bath once a week
our mothers struggled, illness to defeat.

Memories of the fear I felt at night
crossing the yard to the privy without light.
When winter came, and the water pipes froze
cold seemed to freeze my very bones.

Children who survived those severe years
appreciate our mothers' loving care.
Without their fighting tenacity
a barren land, this would have been.

The toll in stress and health was great
alone the mothers in this war waged.
Honoured by none, but we who remember
whose survival was mothers' only agenda.

Evelyn Poppy Sawyer

BALLAD OF THE HIGHLAND WARRIORS

I dreamed I stood in a Scottish glen
And I heard the songs of the Highland men,
I heard the pipes play a sad lament
But I could not see which way they went.

Then borne on the wind from over the brae
I heard a battle cry far away,
The claymores clashed and a cannon roared,
I heard the yells of a seething horde.

I dreamed I stood in a Scottish glen,
And I saw the ghosts of the Highland men,
Their kilts gaily swinging to and fro
As they marched from the battle they fought long ago.

Pauline M Parlour

GYPSY

Dark and dusty, brown-skinned maiden
Letting fall the modern modes,
With your arms and pockets laden,
Not for you the dyes and wodes.

A pannier of wild stinging nettles
Found and from the brown earth gathered
And before the eagle settles
Made to where you van is tethered.

All the natural world's before you
Not for you the packaged chicken,
And you know the world adores you,
Envies you your fields and lichen.

Bare feet treading on the brown earth,
Hair unstyled and flowing free.
I'd give you my life and its worth
To roam as you 'neath sky and tree.

Joan Elizabeth Blissett

RULER OF THE COIN

The farthing spoke not to the wren,
As it said its final goodbye to an old-time friend,
The halfpenny was next into the fold,
They tell me I've got to go too, now I'm getting old.

The captain of the crew, the largest one,
A whole penny, too, soon was gone,
Then along came the threepenny bit,
No hope for me either, they're going to give me a miss.

Then those of silver - born of the crown,
Their turn too, had arrived now,
Soon never to be seen again, our old friend the tanner,
Who decried to treat one of such worth in this manner.

Long gone the crown, mother of the family,
Now its younger child, only half its age, too must leave,
'And what of me?' asked the shilling,
Well, you're going to be known as ten pence, that's if you're willing.

In hiding too, was the florin, the old two bob,
'What's in store for me? Have I got a new job?'
The ten shilling and pound notes, likewise the same,
Had heard that they'd never be made of paper, ever again.

A new ruler had arrived to take over the land,
And place unknown coins of worth into each and every hand,
Decimalisation - not a king or queen,
Was to change forever, that which once had been.

Richard H Bennett

MYSTICAL ECSTASY - TULIP

Swim the Sea of Mamara,
Swim it for Triumph to reach Samsara!
Planting flowers in rich river gardens:
Fertile hearts to cover heads, wear turbans.

Sultan wrote poems in great reverence,
Names to honour lover in deference:
'O, My Beloved', 'Light Of Your Eyes' colour -
Sorrow if something withered our ardour!

Lustful folly of full moon in April,
Flower festival: Istanbul Tulip
Play rhapsody on a lyre: a turtle
Saunters by, caged birds sing to the candle

Borne on its back. Some mystical emblem
(Amsterdam's first diamond) surreal gem:
This soft sensation of pleasure flower
Before avaricious heat of summer.

Pomegranate - kiss apple full of seeds
But this species dies Dutch economy
Where the bulbs had been sold for title deeds!
Yet the flower is still beautiful ecstasy.

Suzanne Stratful

HORSEPLAY

Whilst driving in my taxi car
I saw a golfer potting par
'What's strange?' you ask, as well you might
'Twas in the middle of the night

He swung his club, and shouted 'Fore'
Success is less, not round in more
This ghostly golfer in misty shroud
Birdied his eagle, and was proud

I stopped my car, got out to see
This apparition on the tee
But as I struggled through the gorse
I trod in something left by horse

He swished his tail and whinnied more
'I'd have pulled your cab in days of yore'
I asked 'Why are you on the course?'
He said 'Can't speak, I'm feeling hoarse.'

He searched around without avail
For something missing 'neath his tail
The first of horse in ballad's form
Anagram, 'less' than when first born

The mystery now is plain to all
Why grown men hit a little ball
Whilst walking through a field of grass
With nothing more than time to pass

Bill Hodgson

BALLAD OF THE PRODIGAL

A son did want to leave his home,
And wander far away.
His father gave him chance to roam
And find a brighter day.

For long he did enjoy himself
In a far off country,
But soon he'd squandered all his wealth.
He'd spent all his bounty.

Poor was he, and all alone.
His friends had left in fright.
His empty stomach made a groan.
He was an awful sight.

He got a job a-feeding pigs,
The lowest of the low.
This home not like his previous digs,
He missed his father so.

At last he swallowed all his pride
And trundled back again.
His nerves were really ripped inside
Would this be in vain?

But Father's welcome always stood
He loved his dear child.
He always did just what he could
E'en though his child was wild.

The father told his other son
In midst of jubilation,
That now they all would live as one
And have a celebration.

Judith Thomas

POETRY

A song of the soul
And balm to the heart,
A theme for each mood
And thought for the art.

The pleasure of words,
The rhythms that tease,
The magic of each
Is needed to please.

So, read to one's self
Or heard by us all,
We thrill at the thought,
Are held in its thrall.

Eileen Shenton

I HAD A DREAM

I had a dream, when I was young,
When days were full of things to come.
All roads unknown, all songs unsung,
First careless love, not yet begun.

Like a shining path, life lay ahead
Unknown, untrodden, a book unread.
My future lay where fortune led -
I dreamed my dream, until my youth had fled.

I lived my life and fought my fight,
Tried to do what was fair and right.
Loved my love with a love so bright
Close to my heart, in the still of the night.

The years go by, I found my dream
Remembering the glorious world I've seen,
The songs I've sung, the places I have been,
The silver spell of the moon's bright beam.

Memories recalled, forever, it seems
Locked in my heart, safe in my dreams.

Betty Leyster Justice

BIRTHDAY WISH

Happy Birthday to you dear
may flowers strew your way,
and all the birds that fly above
sing gladly thro' the day.
May gentle breezes softly blow
the leaves on every tree,
and shake the cobwebs from your eyes
that all God's gifts you see.
May stars above shine down at night
where shadows softly fall,
and may your day be full of joy,
as pleasures you recall.

Maimie Watson Stokoe

A LOVELY DAY

On such a lovely day my soul rejoices
The blue sky and the sun uplift my heart
The birds sing out their songs with happy voices
The blossom and the flowers their scents impart.

Just lately spring has worn a miserable disguise
The heavy rain and wind depressed the soul
But God above has plans and he is wise
And all the different weathers play out their role.

January, February and all their winter cold
With March and April rough winds and heavy showers.
But patience is rewarded as days of May unfold
Making merry are the insects, birds and flowers.

Feel the soft warm breeze and the sun upon your face
Smell the perfume, hear the sounds of summer on its way
Let your senses have the pleasure, absorb it, drink it in
Be happy and rejoice in this lovely day.

A Heathershaw

SUMMER OF LOVE

So pleasant, the sunshine-filled days,
The heady scent of spices on the breeze,
Castaways on our island of love,
Capturing fond memories.

The sundrenched world we are among,
Seascapes, sunsets, coral coves,
Sensational we are together having fun,
All of this our first summer of love.

Carnival delights, to dance the night away,
Exotic sights of our holiday,
The great atmosphere, the nice places to eat,
What a glorious, special summer retreat.

To embrace it all, the lush scenery,
Pure relaxation in the sounds of the sea,
All of our special sun-filled moments,
Joyfully cherished, in the tides of history.

Natasha Faiers

To Touch The Sky

A flower, blue.
A stem of green.
A sight as splendid as is seen
among the massive snow-capped peaks.
'To touch the sky'
the mountains cry,
As shadows crawl along the floor,
Opening the sparkling door
of night.
Twinkle after twinkle seeks
the next arrival of the throng,
another star.
The distant suns sing out their song.
So bright,
the many points of light.
So far,
the journey to the further scene.
So near as day returns to warm the stem of green,
A drop of dew,
And flower blue.

Athol Cowen

THE SOLDIER'S WORDS

They say he is the Son of God,
Can't see the reason why,
just because he healed the sick,
and was not afraid to die.
Just because the crowds all came
from miles to hear him speak,
and listen while he taught them,
all sat around his feet.
Then cast out demons with a word,
and made the blind to see,
and walked upon the water,
and made the leper clean.
And then he cried 'Forgive them'
as they sentenced him to die.
They say he is the Son of God,
Can't see the reason why.

Ken Price

JOSHUA

Tall and gangly with a long white tail
He barks at the milk and he barks at the mail.
He pulls up the flowers he's ruined our lawn,
Not from this planet. Oh where was he born?

He arrived one Thursday from the RSPCA
My wife said 'I want him. He's here to stay.'
Elizabeth was laughing, she thought it was great,
They gave him some dinner. They gave him *my* plate!

'It took three men to catch him' she stated with glee,
I said 'I don't like him, I'm sure that's a flea.'
'But he's a real pointer, just look at his face.'
'We haven't the money, we haven't the space.'

He pulls on the lead and chases the cat,
Plays with a football till it's punctured and flat.
He begs at the table, he sleeps on the bed,
He finishes our meals, he's much too well fed.

We take him to Filey to play in the sea,
He splashes with Sophie, doesn't need me.
Then he bounds up the beach and gives us a smile,
Turns back to the waves chasing gulls for a while.

He doesn't like trumpet, doesn't like flute,
The children all love him, he really is cute.
Our crazy pal Joshua
In his shiny brown suit.

Michael Needham

HONEY

Have you met our Honey-dog?
She's been with us for years.
Shared with us the happy times,
And helped us through the tears.
When she was young and carefree,
On long legs she would race.
Around the fields and beach and lanes,
Eagerness upon her face.
Now her pace is slower,
She doesn't often run,
She likes to lie beside the fire,
Or in the garden in the sun.
From lively pup to grand old lady,
We know her years are numbered,
Her eyes are dim, her ears are weak,
With old age she's encumbered.
Honey, much loved and faithful girl,
Such times with you we have spent,
We hope we've made you happy,
Comfortable and content.
Thank you, Honey, for being you,
For loving us each day,
For lots of lovely memories,
To take with us on life's way.

Joy Cooke

BETTY'S TARTAN TREWS

The day that Betty bought her trews
To wear on Arnold's river cruise,
The salesgirl, skilled in every ruse,
Offered our Bet some high-heeled shoes
And asked her for some simple clues
As to what she had in mind to choose.
'Well,' said Bet, 'a pair with vibrant hues,
A striking blend of reds and greens and blues;
A pair that would light a fuse
Under an elderly eunuch. Excuse
The image, but no man willingly woos
A girl who covers up and fails to use
Her natural advantages. Don't accuse
Me of being timid: win or lose,
I want a vivid tartan and I don't care whose.'

The day that Betty wore her trews
Oh what a treat for the unsuspecting crews
Out to enjoy the Thames-side views!
How could they possibly refuse
To shift their gaze from the graceful yews
And shaded well-constructed avenues
To focus now on Bet's curvaceous thews.
And such the effect of the spreading news
That thirsty chaps forsook their booze
Or other more sophisticated brews;
While some awoke from pleasant snooze,
And others left unfinished stews
Prepared to join, in British style, the queues
Of those who, having seen, could only muse:
Is it the Loch Ness monster? One of Swift's Yahoos?
Or something crept from earth's primeval ooze?

The day that Betty split her trews . . .

William R Braide

A STURDY TWO-SEATER

Marriage is a vehicle made for two
At its conception sparkling like innocent dew
Two ideas of life joined in a band of gold
Newly smooth - worn with experience as it grows old
The knocks and scrapes glint as imperfections
With understanding both see their own reflections
A little rub and mutual respect polishes both
Whilst living and loving they experience growth
Change can be painful but loneliness is death
With patience they arrive at a place that is blessed
Two old souls who have travelled the road
In a vehicle whose strength supports and enfolds
It may be outdated but still living proof
Of a fuel called love and the wheels of truth.

Brenda Dove

DREAMS

I looked up and saw you
Your eyes shining bright
You reached for my hand
And we danced with the night

We bounced over mountains
And ran through the vales
Or we'd just lay for hours
Into moonlight we sailed

We conquered the world
In just over a day
A tear in my eye
As I begged you to stay

I asked you to marry
As you sat on my bed
And the very next day
You said yes, and we wed

You were so handsome
So pure and so right
So strange, yet my lover
That came in the night

And I'll always love you
My heart sings your song
But in the morning I'll wake up
And once again, you'll be gone.

Karen Churchward

NEW LOVE

People will say he's wrong for you!
Before they even meet him
He'll be damned;
Without having to greet him
He'll be doomed.
Always that mantra
When you meet someone new,
People will claim
He's not worthy of you.
When winter branches antler the sky
Folk will challenge, *Him!*
But why, oh why?
Even your fair-weather counsellor
With that hippopotamus smile
Warns against the dangers
Of wile and guile,
Of interloper summer strangers
Who land then fly away,
Enthralling you by just
Living for the day,
Blinding your chance of tomorrows
As if yesterdays weren't for sorrows.
Beware that false litany
When you love someone new,
Some folk will insist
He's not good enough for you!

Malcolm Williams

THE LURE OF THE SEA

A call is borne on the summer breeze,
A call that reaches my heart,
A call that is whispered amid the trees,
When the leaf-laden branches part.

'Tis the call of the sea from far away
In another enchanting land,
Where the waves are murmuring all the day
On the sand.
Where the white gulls swoop and wheel and cry,
Skimming the glistening foam,
Where the sea is the same soft blue as the sky,
There is my home.
And sometimes the wind is racing along,
Hurling the waves on the shore,
And the sound of the sea and wind is a song
That lingers for evermore.

The scent of the sea and the soft, warm rain,
Are calling me, calling me,
Back to the land of my home again,
Back to the restless sea.

Joan Letts

KIND THOUGHTS

I'm thinking of you
I know that you are feeling blue
I would like you to cheer up, feel free
Live life as it is meant to be.

It's time to come over, learn how to play
It is by talking you'd drive your tears away
I can bake a cake, perhaps buy some scones
Maybe take the car for a run, have fun.

You'll always find a friend in me
I'd like to be close, as close as can be
As sisters we lived and played
There is no need to be dismayed.

I am there for you
As I hope you'll be there for me.
Ready to share our burdens as they arise
And together we will reach the sky.

Doris Morrison

GOD'S GIFT

If there had been no Christ Child on that first Christmas Day,
If angels had not visited the shepherds where they lay;
Suppose the star had not appeared, bright in the eastern sky,
Wise Men would not have travelled or even questioned why!
If Christ had not been born that day, just stop and think awhile,
What would it mean to you and I with non to reconcile?
We'd have no hope, no future, no cure for human pain,
We'd sing no joyful carols with their happy glad refrain.
If Jesus Christ had not been born, there'd be no Calvary,
There'd be no cross, no empty tomb; no one to set us free.
But Christ did come a babe so small that starry Christmas night,
And angels told the shepherds, who rejoiced with great delight.
They came to Bethlehem and saw, God's wondrous gift was given
To all mankind, and from that day the gates of Hell were riven.
So let us too rejoice with them and let our praises ring,
And with the shepherds let us bow and worship Christ the King.

Andrea Macrow

THE GERMAN RETREAT IN EASTERN AND WESTERN EUROPE

The Russians were defeating the Germans in nineteen-forty-three,
The Germans retreated in mass to Berlin's country;
Eric Von Straffenberg was part of a plot,
Who unsuccessfully tried to assassinate Hitler's murdering lot.
Operation Overlord was then created and from England
To beyond the beaches of France and sand;
It involved all the allied forces in power,
And was commanded by the American Ike Eisenhower.
The leaders American General Patton with his call,
English Field Marshall Montgomery and French General de Gaulle;
Helped to push the Germans back to Berlin,
One German wished that he was Magic Merlin.
As the retreat reached the forests of Germany,
The German army launched themselves a motorised harmony;
A counter-attack of tough Tiger tanks in deceit,
Created the Battle of the Bulge's American retreat.
After a while, the Tiger tanks were defeated,
In the battle by burning fuel being heated;
Whilst Japanese conquests were being counter-attacked and liberated,
American marine forces were liberating Guadualcanal, Japanese hated.

Ian K A Ferguson

Our Holiday In Swanage

I was feeling rather blue because money was short
And I wanted a holiday, but didn't think I ought.
Then Mum suggested taking me away
So both of us would get a holiday.
We went through the book and this suited us,
So I phoned and reserved it without any fuss.
As the time for travelling drew quite near
I planned out a route to get us here.
With one short diversion the journey went well,
We arrived at reception and rang the bell.
They made us very welcome and gave us a key,
A room downstairs for Mum, and upstairs for me.
Since arriving there, has been lots to see
As well as a ramble 'around the world' for me.
We have walked on the prom and I've paddled in the sea
Driven through the country where the best things are free.
The birds and animals, sunshine and flowers,
Trees meet overhead to make shady bowers.
Peace and beauty for all to see
And shared this summer by Mum and me.

Lynne Walden

NEW BEGINNING

Today is the start of a new beginning,
    when hurt and anger fade away
When a heart that's numbed by cold rejection
    can hope for the warmth of a sun's new day
When hope can find a new direction
    unhindered by love's dying throes
Unfettered dreams lay disregarded
    making way as a new dream grows
When a heart that's crushed,
    and a spirit, beaten,
Can rise from where in pain they lay
    and softly, gently with love's understanding
Turn, for warmth to the sun's new day.

Today is the start of a new beginning
    born of tears, of hurt and pain
Born of a need of an understanding
    love, that's fanned by compassion's flame
Born of the need of a true companion
    to be, for me, my whole life's aim
Born of a faith that's badly shaken,
    of love and trust, few illusions remain,
Born of a need to love and be loved
    My love is dead, let me love again!

Liz Allsworth

ONE DAY IN THE DIARY OF A WIDOW

It's Monday again, another week,
It's too much trouble to write,
To liven things up, all I can put,
Is 'The weather is sunny and bright'!
I don't seem to know what to do,
My friend says I should read a good book,
Or make a menu for an interesting meal,
But I burn whatever I cook.
I can't even sew, my stitches are big,
If I turn up and hem, it seems odd,
If I get down on my knees, I look up with pain,
They will think I am praying to God!
I should get on my feet, take a long walk,
Get my lungs filled with all this fresh air,
But after ten minutes, my knees start to ache,
And I'm filled with a sense of despair.
It's no fun getting older and creaking,
When at one time, you've been raring to go,
So don't be too hard on my ramblings,
I'm just a lonely old person you know.
I shouldn't be scribbling this sob stuff,
In this diary I write every day,
But you know what they remark about old folks,
They all like to have a good say!

Edith Antrobus

CROSSROADS - NO SIGNPOSTS

Two old women stood at the crossroads with never a signpost in sight,
In different ways neglected, yet no one knew of their plight,
Why were they allowed to get so old before anyone assisted their state?
For the one her cupboard was empty, for someone had left it too late.
The other took pity on children, until she could 'take no more',
A little forethought could have eased the pain of carrying the
burden she bore.
I'm sure we knew these nursery rhymes and related them to
our children.
Perhaps we're at fault when we 'turn a blind eye',
Hoping the problem will just disappear,
But try as we will, it haunts us still, unless we trouble to care.

Hilary Owens

THE INFLEXIBLE PRINCIPLE

Never deny love.
Deny the ever-spinning Earth is spherical,
That every longitude upon it is numerical.
Assert the latest pop group's not hysterical;
Maintain a hill is flat, the plain a cavity.
And, putting chair to ceiling, refute gravity:
Deny the world is conquered by depravity,
That councils and developers work hand-in-glove:
Never deny love.

Deny your faults: Refute that once you tried
Lysergic acid diethylamide
And, falling from a rainbow, nearly died.
Deny compassion, hatred - and elation
That when you parted from a rich relation
You said, 'Farewell' upon the crowded station
Not with a tender handshake, but a shove.
Never deny love.

Refute, though captured on CCTV,
That you were ever there. Deny all certainty.
Deny you are, and all your right to be:
Though crucified with thorn and sword and nail
Still resolute, let constancy prevail:
Denial is the ultimate betrayal.
Though flung into the endless void above
Never deny love.

Paul de Mapingham

THE LITTLE CHURCH AT EVENSONG

At the end of the lane stood the old grey church
Deep in the shade of a silver birch
Its lonesome bell tolls loud and long
Welcoming all to evensong
A little church loved with gentle care
Peace and tranquillity reigning there
Where the village folk can sit and pray
To ease the burdens of their day
The altar rail of gleaming brass
Windowpanes of latticed glass
Well tended blooms in vases tall
Holy scriptures on the wall
Old Becky Brown in Sunday hat
Is always first - she loves to chat
With everyone who comes along
To the little church for evensong
The village policeman turns to speak
To the farmer's wife with apple cheek
Whilst a mother bursting with much pride
Regards her offspring at her side
Doors opened wide to fading sun
The evening service now begun
Scrubbed choir boys with well-brushed hair
Angelic chanting fills the air
A secret thought in every head
Each glad of the pathway that has led
To the old church bell with message strong
Calling them all to evensong.

Barbara Davies

THE SINGER AND THE SONG

I pause and listen to the song
It falls so sweetly on the ear,
To which glad bird does it belong
And will the singer perhaps appear?

I search around in bush and tree
To find that chorister so sweet.
But hidden he remains from me
My knowledge of him incomplete.

In my heart his happy trill
Still lingers as I take my way,
The pleasure that it gave me will
Remain with me throughout the day.

Barbara L Jones

LITTLE LOST MUM

We cared for our parents, as they cared for us,
We both did the best that we could.
Then Dad died and Mum was left all alone,
Like a little maid lost in a wood.
As time passed we lost our mum more every day,
Her mind, eyes and hearing grew dim.
She searched for her husband, but he'd passed away,
She longed to fly off free with him.
We visited Mum, but she didn't want us,
She'd often not know who we were.
It was tragic to see her dejected, alone.
Just what could we do to help her?
A new day would dawn, we'd waken to wonder
What thoughts were there in our mum's mind.
We'd wake in the night scared that something was wrong,
Just what were we going to find?
Then one day it happened, a hospital stay.
Dehydrated, she'd fallen down.
She could not come home, no more could be done
But residential care near our home town.
We cared for our mother and we miss her so.
We visit, she's not really there.
Her house is sold and to us she is lost.
As long as she lives, we still care.
Now Mum exists in a world of her own
To which we cannot find a door.
She's cared for, she's tended, but left
Wondering just what her existence is for.

Norma Langley

THE MERMAID

I come from the Sea
Fresh blown with the Tide
The incoming flow
Directed my mind -

A Sea Nymph!
Why not?
If Martians can land
I've as much right as they

And popular demand
I would say would elect -
A Mermaid so fair
Than that queer object
Landed in from the Air.

Who knows? - We might merge
In Friendship of Three -
The Martian, the Earthbound,
And the Mermaid - that's me!

Mary Skelton

MOOD STONE

Emotions I keep hidden deep inside.
Emotions that I feel that I must hide.
Emotions that I cannot let you see
Preventing you from ever knowing me.

Emotions that I pray you'll never know.
Emotions that torment my spirit so.
Emotions that forever take their toll
Devouring my body, heart and soul.

Emotions that some just could not believe.
Emotions that you're trying to perceive.
Emotions that you wish to understand.
You place a mood stone in my hand.

Emotions change the stone from hue to hue.
Emotions you never knew you never knew.
Emotions that you see as clear as day
As the mood stone changes from amber to grey.

Emotions that I now can comprehend.
Emotions as my broken heart doth mend.
Emotions that I can't hide any more.
This is really what a mood stone's for.

Emotions, I feel at peace, so serene.
Emotions that make the mood stone light green.
Emotions that control all I say and do.
Emotions. The mood stone proves that they are true.

Louise Fleet

VALENTINE

We can't live together, that's plain
But how can we stand life apart?
We are driving each other insane.
Have we two, or just one breaking heart?

I reach for him now with my mind
Picturing him by the sea
Alone with the sand, sea and sky
Hoping he's reaching for me.

The sea, like our turbulent love,
Hides a deep secret world of its own.
Under those calm waves above
Life and death fight proud battles unknown.

My love has been boiling two years.
Could it boil dry now he has left me?
The wind will dry his salty tears.
Mine still come, mine still come, flowing free.

Where are his candid blue eyes
That penetrate right to the soul,
So changing in mood and in size -
Virgin white, lucid blue, black as coal?

That soft understanding clear look
Said more than a well-prepared speech -
Consoling as music or book,
Condemning, where words couldn't reach.

Everything he's ever said
And everything he's ever done
Will stay like a song in my head
And cling like the love that he's won.

Dorothy

JOY

Come play the music
Tease the heart to dance
Bring back old memories
Of long ago romance.
Strike up the fiddle
So the sound is sweet
Set off the rhythm
For any tapping feet.
All human souls respond
To merry tuneful air
Spirits they are lifted high
Beyond the realms of care.
So come play the music
Once again to hear
Melodies we loved so well
In happy yesteryear.

Marion P Webb

YOUTH

All young are inquisitive
They want to know a lot,
No matter what the cost to them,
Or if the water's hot.

Youth rebels with orders
It does its own thing,
And comes a cropper doing it
Yet still has cause to sing!

Yet, inside every OAP
There's a youngster peering out
Watching all of modern youth.
At times they want to shout,
Can I try out that skateboard?
Do a wheelie on your bike?
Can I borrow Charlie's Walkman
For the fund raising hike?
It looks smashing on that surfboard,
A microlight seems fun!

If only they could pass the test
On an MOT run!

Zoë Ford

My Daughter

I have a wonderful daughter
She was wonderful from day one
Her hair was a beautiful red
That shone when touched by the sun
And as she grew into a teenager
She became a normal raver
But her beauty, kindliness and love
Was always there as if from Heaven above
I taught her right from wrong
And made her feel she always belonged
And when I look at us today
No one can take that love away
We love and respect each other
Every single day.

Joy Willoughby

A LIFE STORY

I threw away my bucket and spade,
When my childhood began to fade,
As I reached my early teens
My heart was full of hopeful dreams.
I would become a superstar
But that would never go very far.
When I hit the big two O,
What on earth was there for me now?
Nine till five, twenty-four seven
Will I ever get out for eleven?
There came a day I released two doves
For this was the day that I found love.
Two beautiful children did I raise
Through many of our wonderful days.
Now years have vanished with the past
I know my memories will always last.
My walking stick in my hand
My legs could barely stand.
When I look back at what used to be
How grand has life been to me.

Jolene Neary

DAY TRIPPER

Everyone went - including me
On Day Tripper Trains
For a day by the sea.
Macs packed for rain,
Spam butties for tea,
It was always the same
On those trips to the sea.

Queuing for tickets - including me
For Day Tripper Trains
En route for the sea.
Dodging the rain,
Fish and chip tea
It was always the same
On our trips to the sea.

Everyone went - including me
On Bank Holiday Trains
For a day by the sea.
Pouring with rain,
Afternoon tea,
It was always the same
On day trips to the sea.

Kids 'I spied' and 'Oxoed' - including me
On steam powered trains
On our trips to the sea.
Macs packed for rain,
Spam butties for tea,
It was always the same
On those trips to the sea.

Betty Lightfoot

SUMMER OF FLOWERS

Summer comes in a blaze of flowers
With long, long days and hot sunny hours.
There are flowers in baskets and in wheelbarrows
Flowers on beans - flowers on marrows!

They're blooming here, they're blooming there
Flowers are blooming everywhere!
Brightest of blooms to offset the duller
Florid scenes of all shapes and colour.

The bees enjoy their blossomed treat -
Above the rustic garden seat.
The meadow 'tis a child's delight
With scarlet poppies o' so bright!

As glorious summer passes on -
Flowers get fewer, then they're gone
And through the leafless garden bowers
Ripe fruits blossom in place of flowers.

On window sill in curtained bay
Stands summer's precious last bouquet
And drying by the gardening manuals
Reclaimed seeds for next year's annuals!

Norah Page

WHAT WOULD IT BE LIKE TO BE A BIRD?

I stand in the garden,
listening to the birds.
I'd love to talk to them,
but I don't know the words.
They sing a lovely song,
not a single note is wrong.
They're sitting in a tree,
as happy as can be.
Then they flutter and they fly,
so high into the sky.
They swerve and they curve . . .
What would it be like to be a bird?

Alexandra Nicholson-Evans

THE ROSE

No flower is more lovely than the rose
In the English garden it widely grows
It can be a bush, a rambler or a tree
Whatever, its blossoms are such beauty to see

In shades of white, yellow or crimson red
No other flower has so much been said
Petals like heavy silk, that drape and fold
To the breeze its fragrance does behold

Such heavenly scent lingering, on the night air
To let us know, that it still remains there
Dark shiny leaves on a stem of thorn
Please do not pick me, it seems to warn

Steeped in history this wondrous flower
The Wars of the Roses held mighty power
The flower of love to a woman from a man
The rose is the national emblem of our land

Painted by artists and much written in verse
A gracious flower that holds no curse
The 'Queen of Flowers' the crown doth wear
So lovely is the rose, it will always be there

Linda Brown

EVENTIDE

Leisurely I wandered in the quiet evening hour,
The Earth was fragrant and refreshed after a gentle shower.
The raindrops sparkled on the grass like countless diamonds bright,
The whole world seemed illumined by the sun's warm golden light.

The sunbeams shimmered on the lake where swallows were
a-skimming,
And there I paused to watch a swan effortlessly swimming,
Presently some cattle came down to the water's brink,
And waded in the shallows to take a cooling drink.

The tall white chestnut blossoms shone clearly through the shade
Which their embowering foliage in vivid contrast made,
The lilac and the hawthorn with their fragrance filled the air,
A sense of quiet contentment hovered round me everywhere.

The shadows lengthened as the sun sank slowly in the west,
And Mother Nature gently lulled her little ones to rest,
And there amidst the sweetness and the deep tranquillity,
Amidst the soul refreshing beauty, surely God walked there with me.

N Tudor

I KNOW A PLACE

I know a *place* - a wondrous *sweet secret place*
A silent nectarine valley of mystic offering
Spreading green sward fingers toward outer space
Absorbing strength from all nature's elements proffering.

Each Summer dawn, subtly, serene and gently
A circumcision of light from darkness occurs
Suffusing, to reveal metal sky eventually
Later converting to dappled sunspot on meadow and firs.

As Autumn nudges Winter, and hanging dewdrops turn to ice
My *wondrous sweet secret place* becomes alive with phosphor glow
Summer verdant colours are seen adjusting in a trice
In a few short weeks there'll be a surplice of snow.

Oh *wondrous sweet secret place,* where man's heart desires come true
Where supine dreaming can persuade fiction into fact
And powerful love forces work - of every kind of hue
Leave me to tarry, letting spirit heal intact.

The Good Lord above gave me knowledge of *this place*
My own magic *bailiwick* to seek out when forlorn
Don't try to follow it, my footsteps you'll *never* trace
Unless you feel as I feel - *many worldly things to scorn.*

I guarantee you'll not find my *secret place* - few people ever do
Unless you prove beyond all doubt nature's magic doth enthral
Most folk live their whole lives through
Never ever finding it *not in Summer nor in Fall.*

Paul Harvey Jackson

76

ENGLISH SKIES FOR ME

The smell of the earth after rain
As flowers are born again.
The drops their petals gently shake
These my picture of England make.

When the cloud, so heavy and grey
Has gone speedily on its way
The brilliant blue takes its place
And each shining flower turns its face

To the clear, bright sun.
A heavenly painting, sweetly done.
Backed by many greens, of shrubs and trees,
Its gentleness made to please.

Not for me the gaudy blaze
Of that same sun in foreign ways,
Where even the flowers' colours glare
And humans, in sunglasses stand and stare

At flaunting reds and orange hues
Which give no rest . . . no I would choose
A fickle sun which plays with rain
Peeping, hiding, then out again.

Fields which are watered, their crops made green,
Where my eyes rest on views, which when seen
In an English light, can swiftly change
Their charm, and through the spectrum range.

How tedious it would be
If day after day we would see
Only bright blue skies with never a cloud, but burning sun.
O! English skies, my heart have won.

Deirdre White

A HOUSEWIFE

A housewife's job's not much fun
From morn till night when day is done,
Scrubbing floors, and washing dishes
Filling all the family's wishes,
Making beds and doing sewing
Seeing that the bills aren't owing.
Now what shall we have for dinner?
My the purse is getting thinner.
Hustle, bustle, all the day,
Lots of work, not much pay.
Feeling weary, maybe glum
Till a 'voice' says 'Hello Mum.'
Dad and daughter then big brothers,
Aren't we glad we're wives and mothers?
As they greet you with a smile
Then the day seems all worthwhile.

Joan Patrickson

FRIENDSHIP

Friendship is precious
Friendship is rare
It's loving and giving
And learning to share

To listen with understanding
Your friend's point of view
And help them whatever
The cost is to you

To learn to be patient
Loving and kind
And to share all your worries
You keep locked in your mind

A true friend will listen
And never repeat or pass on
True friendship will last
After others have gone

And over the years
If you move far away
Send letters or phone her
Remember her birthday

Things that mean so little
Can mean such a lot
When you are remembered
For yourself
Not the things you have got

Stella Hughes

POPPIES

Seas of poppies sway blood red
Amid the lush green meadows,

Young and old, by the score,
Through the meadow . . . once marched to war,

Songs they sang to pass the time,
Comrades now . . . in step and rhyme

Hark the sound of distant guns,
Keep marching . . . marching . . . one by one!

Thunderous tanks and battle guns,
Ant-like soldiers . . . beside it run.

Heads up lads, shoulders back,
Sergeant's shout, through smoke grey-black!

A thunderous noise, and all is still,
No more the sound of voices,

One by one they fall about,
Lie low. Lie low . . . their comrades shout

Too late . . . amid the bloodied mud
So still the bodies lie.

An eerie silence falls like mist
Will next the bullet, be *hit* or *miss!*

Husbands, father, brother's sons!
For them their duty . . . now is done!

Rank and file, the list is long,
For those who died . . . no victory songs!

Forget not I . . . of those who died
Too young was I, to stand beside.

Poppy now . . . I wear with pride,
A symbol for all . . . that fought and died!

Seas of poppies sway blood red
Amid . . . the lush green meadows.

Sylvia Connor

THE CASTLE ON DEVIL'S ISLAND

Upon an old, deserted hill, where no bird ever sings,
Remains the ancient castle where dwelt the island's kings;
This castle once was beautiful, or so we have been told -
So many happy tales abound of its golden days of old
Until the last king reigned there, and how dreadful were those days -
The carefree times were over and the isle knew evil ways:

This king made many enemies whilst he disgraced the throne
For nobody could please him as his heart was made of stone:
Deep down into the dungeons his visitors he'd take
Where sweet-tongued birds would lull them to slumber, ne're to wake!
His ending is unknown to us, there's nothing left to show
How he and death met face-to-face so many years ago.

The island's not inhabited by people any more,
But snakes and lizards live there, and gorillas by the score!
Once known as 'Eden's Garden', the isle has changed its name
And 'Devil's Island' suffers from disreputable fame;
None dares to go to Castle Hill when vanished is the light,
For evil fate will come to all who trespass there at night!

Rosemary Y Vandeldt

ENTREATIES

Will you give me your warmth?
For far gone is the day
And chill the night wind,
Oh please do not delay.

Cut off was my spring,
My summer despoiled,
My autumn so saddened
Can my winter be foiled?

Will you give me your gentleness
Which others refuse
That comfort I may take
As upon life I muse?

The night has much darkness
Amidst moon's glimmer of light.
The true path can I find again
And become free of the blight?

Will you give me your kindness
In this world hard as stone,
Where courage is needed
As I focus on home?

Long gone is my youth,
I look back with dismay
On disappointments mid tumult
I must cling to the way.

Will you give me your love now
As you did in years long past?
For if of that I am worthy
Rest will I find at last.

Jeffrey Owen

LIFE CONNECTION

The sacred link between
Man and earth
Is forged at the moment
Of birth.

With the first breath of life
The connection is made
A bond that will last
For all of our days.

From the fresh green of spring
To days of summer gold
These are the joys that are ours
To behold.

The icy hues of winter blue
With colours from nature's store
The link remains our whole life through
Until the end when we return
To Mother Earth once more.

Carole Harradence

OUR ROCK

Two years have now gone since you left us
When a kind gentle man passed away
Those years have just seemed like minutes
And, we've counted them, right down to the day
We've missed everything that you stood for
An intelligent and witty man
One who was in the Airforce
Who found missiles, destroyed them and ran
You have told us many a story
Of some of the things you have done
The disasters you've had to get through
But you did it, you triumphed and won
To us you were our salvation
You were there when things were so bad
You helped us all back to recovery
You were a wonderful husband and dad
We thought of you very highly
For you guided us all every day
And now sometimes we're just drifting
And we stumble and can't find our way
We all wish we could have you back again
For your death it was such a shock
You were always our all and everything
A husband, our father, our rock.

Alison Taylor

THINGS

Buy it, wrap it, send it back.
Broken, damaged, hair-line crack,
Spoiled, wrecked discarded thing,
Bring and buy and buy and bring.
Grandmother's heirloom, pot for growing,
Grandfather's medal, mother's ruin,
War memorial, Cenotaph,
Three-legged donkey, gold giraffe.
You borrowed that a year ago,
I want it back, antique you know.
Come and see the bag of loot,
Browse around the Sunday boot.
Precious thing, worthless rubbish,
I've started bidding so I'll finish.
It belongs to me, here's proof of sale,
Tale to tell, so tell the tale.
Broken, damaged, hair-line crack,
Buy it, wrap it, send it back.
Bring and buy and buy and bring,
Spoiled, wrecked, discarded thing.

Elizabeth Hopkinson

TOLERANCE

Tolerance needed as life is a toil,
  The older folk get the brisker their boil,
Obstructions appearing wherever you turn,
  Language a'brewing, as screeched tyres burn.
Loyalty, flaking away from a call,
  Eager for response, a temper most raw.
Everyone else that surrounds is at fault,
  Written in expression, sarcastic insults.
Registrar's, lawyers, a barrister's say,
  Answers required, without slightest delay.
Ample notification is few,
  Cancellation, starts adrenaline to brew.
Near to surrender, as young voices, bawl,
  Firmly but calm, time to tell them, once more.
Conquer the feelings, persist in the task,
  Struggling fourth, through grey shadows, cast.
Extreme is the temper, patience the strife;
  lerance, part of everyday life.

Sara Russell
(Golden Eagles MCC)

FREEDOM'S SONG

I want to break free
Break free of the past,
And enter the future
With new life to last.

I need to break free
And discover myself.
To tackle the problems
I put on the shelf.

I must needs break free
And make a new start.
To learn about me
And what's in my heart.

I have to break free
And throw out the old.
I want to be nice,
Assured and bold.

I know I'll break free.
I shall find me at last.
And when I have strength
I shall learn from the past.

So get out of the way
You faithless self-doubters.
Will-power's returned,
I'm joining the winners!

J G Ryder

AN ARTIST'S LAMENT

My suitcase awaits in the hall,
Water-colours, paint and much more,
First dawn echoes alarm call,
Early morning start always a bore.
A new day is dawning,
Blue skies and seas await me,
But grey clouds overshadow the sun.
The stutter of the engine evokes
Splutters of annoyance and more.
But my suitcase still awaits in the hall,
And breakdown are still out on call.
And still I'm going nowhere,
For my easel's too tall,
So my suitcase which remains in the hall,
Will be hung on a wall, so tall,
And be a constant reminder to one and all
Of the day you walked out of my life,
Forgetting that you are both a mother and a wife.

So with each new day that you are away,
I will rise and walk tall,
But my blue skies and seas,
Will be nothing but trees,
As my suitcase awaits in the hall.

Susan A Peach

HOLIDAYS

The thought of holidays conjure up a sunset beach and a life of luxury
Although it's only going to be a week or two, sheer heaven it's
                                                going to be
I think some years ago we took a break not just because we were bored
In fact to fly half round the world we just could not afford
Some people's idea of holiday is to drive almost until they drop
And although some of the family's not enjoying it the driver doesn't
                                                want to stop
It seems to me that for many, life is lived at such a pace
That even pleasurable pursuits that they seek are almost like a race
A holiday surely should give one the opportunity to relax
But it seems when you get to the chosen venue you could be ready
                                                to collapse
You spend some time getting to the airport and checking out your flight
But you find it's delayed so you wait in the lounge sometimes into
                                                the night
At last you're called that all is well and you're at least on your way
But of the one or two whose holidays end up with disaster
Many thousands enjoy it all - a sort of memories ever after
Some people go on holiday when things go wrong and to get away
                                                from life
But life is what we make it and the break won't help if there is strife
If you're content with someone your life is more or less complete
You do not need exotic holidays in order to compete
If you have some time away it's not to improve your lot
It will be just an extension of what you've already got
So before you take your holiday get reasons right, it needn't be
                                                too grand
In fact with children in particular, all they may want most is just
                                                a square of sand

Reg Morris

THE WIFE

Margaret is a woman
a lass who is sixty-three,
A lass who married at twenty-nine
guess what she married me.
Many years her I have known
to my heart she has the key,
Except when she is on the telephone
speaking for eternity,
A lass with a heart of gold
she gives me her hand to take hold
when crossing the street
or walking down the road,
When together friends we often meet
do not go far now as it is hard on the feet,
In the past children she had
two girls and two lads,
A girl and a boy to heaven went away
grief and sadness is felt to this day,
At five foot high and fifteen stone
a fair complexion with grey hair,
I am six foot two and very stout
so we make the perfect pair,
Finding it hard to make ends meet
on day trips we go for a treat,
We travel some days far and wide
but back home at night to abide,
Though she moans and groans all day
I never do right, I am always wrong,
For me at night I hear her pray
and for her only do I long.

A R Kemp

THE SEA

Without the sea where would we be?
What shape the continents?
We could not stand on cliff or sand
And sense its permanence.

Its fluid robe forms patterned globe
And wraps around our nation;
Without it islands would belie
Their very appellation.

The land would stretch without an edge,
A journey meaningless;
The searching soul would reach no goal,
No constant timelessness.

The swelling breakers rise to make
Us stand and stare, hypnotic;
On land is nowhere motion so
Compellingly dramatic.

Likewise by night the moon's white light,
Uniquely atmospheric
On moving water, nature's law
On land can never mimic.

A gliding gull, a hazy hull,
Expansive sun-specked ocean.
On land-locked ball we'd miss it all
And lack some deep emotion.

Where would we be without the sea,
A gift of providence!
So, tang in nose and sand in toes
We praise its permanence.

Janet Forrest

A Bird In The Hand

Oh pigeon how I love to see
You soaring in the sky
But best of all I'd like you
Sitting in a pie

See brightly coloured pheasants
In the early morning dew
But best of all I'd like you
Sitting in a stew

Rabbits and their young ones
Cute bunnies on the hop
But best of all I'd like you
With a dumpling sat on top

Little deer go running
Through the fields, so young and fine
But best of all I'd like you
Braised in some red wine

If the tables then were turned
And they looked at me instead
I wonder if they'd like me best
Grilled upon some bread!

J Johnson

TALES OF REPENTANCE

Too long I had wandered the dark paths of sin,
I wouldn't let Jesus, the Saviour come in,
He knocked and He pleaded, outside my heart's door,
But I turned Him away, refused Him once more.

The world was inviting and calling me on,
To join with the crowd, on life's busy throng.
Too busy enjoying the pleasures of sin,
In my search to find peace and contentment within.

Even though I had chosen, to go my own way,
Still Jesus kept calling to me and He'd say,
'My child, come with me and turn from your sin,
I can give you that peace and contentment within.'

My friends on the broad road, marvelled to see,
A great transformation happening to me,
I found myself drawing closer to Him,
And no more I yearned for the pleasure of sin.

Then a vision before me I plainly could see,
Of Jesus the Saviour, dying for me.
I fell to my knees, and I cried out in shame,
Then in tears of repentance to Jesus I came.

Oh dear sinner friend, if He's calling today,
Respond to His call, and do not delay,
For unless you repent, and be saved by His grace,
In heaven you won't be assured of a place.

At last I've found peace and contentment within,
And no more I'll travel the broad road of sin.
I'm doing a service for Jesus the King,
I'll search for the lost souls, and bring them to Him.

Shirley Snowden

THOSE THREE LITTLE WORDS

Our relationship is over
I've cried and cried
He's no longer with me
No longer by my side.

'Those words' he said
I'll never forgive
I'm so ashamed
I don't want to live.

His apology' I'm sorry.
Goes around in my brain.
But I *can't* forget
I tell him again and again.

I used to be happy
Until he said 'that'
Those three little words . . .
'You're getting fat'

Brenda Mulls

THE LOOKING GLASS

Come through the looking glass with me,
There are so many lands we want to see,
We don't fly or go by sea, we are there -
As soon as we walk through we see beauty everywhere,
I go to a different place every time I dust,
It takes me a long time but it is a must,
The blue, blue sky, and the tropical flowers,
Amidst all the beauty I spend many hours,
When I have finished everything gleams,
But it is not so beautiful as the things I have seen,
I have dressed in silks and been kissed by a Prince,
I sigh happily as I smooth down my old print,
How happy one can really be, when one escapes from reality,
Just let your imagination wander up, up and away,
While you do your chores from day to day,
The looking glass is a wonderful place,
Where you can see more than just your face.

Jan Graver-Wild

Envy Me?

Two little butterflies,
Near the end of July,
Frantically courting,
As I tiptoed by.

They might've been red admirals,
But they didn't care.
Their total oblivion
Stopped them seeing me there.

Their heady courtship dance
Led them in and out the grass,
She was all a-flutter,
Each time he made a pass.

Round and round the thistles,
Their flight carried on.
As their passion rose higher,
The warm sun shone.

I thought, 'How lucky they are,
That their love won't die,
Since their lives will be over,
In the blink of an eye.

Yet I don't envy them
Their short life span.
For humans want to live
Just as long as they can.

So I wonder if these butterflies
Envy me,
Knowing I write good,
Rhyming poetry?'

Lorna Lea

In Favour Of Rhyming Poetry!

I don't know what it is some people find
In poetry that doesn't rhyme or flow,
That intellectual stuff that stuns the mind
And seems to just be written for the show:
Contemporary, modernistic verse
Supposedly poetic in its form,
Up to the minute, avant-garde and terse
But bound to take the publishers by storm!
Some's excellent, and when I can digest it,
I'll read it in the bath, and over tea:
A lot though, leaves me cold and I detest it
Because it's not poetic. Not to me!

Bring back to us these topsy-turvy times,
The poem that is pleasant, and which rhymes!

Nicholas Winn

FRIENDS

A mind set back
A million years
No progress in his eyes
A life so cheap
And yet so dear
Held in his deep disguise

A winning smile
A knowing look
So easy to submit
Be gentle in your nastiness
To know him
Lights were lit

What epitaph to set before
Those loved ones
So sincere
How strange he'd say
With a confused look
Now he's gone you want him here.

In the final throws
Of life's trick dice
A few points of which to note
Keep your conscience still
Your mind at rest
Keep his memory afloat.

Paul Davis

PATH TO DESTRUCTION - THE BOREDOM SECT

'So undeniably stupid' motivation cried
when driven on by hedonism the
pleasure-seeker died.

'Quite unbelievably foolish' sensible agreed
'to think that such frivolity
to peril would not lead'

'Oh too true' said told-you-so
'my words went quite unheeded'
as onwards to destruction recklessly
he speeded.

'Oh why did he do it?' said reproachable regret
'why could he not be more like us
and join the boredom sect?'

Elizabeth Read

THE MUSIC OF MY HEART

Where is the pleasure of the fleeting year?
Each month is like December all year round,
Where once was faith there is but only fear.
We walked on air where now is ice-cold ground.
The Spring has passed me by; I still am cold.
In summer months no heat can humour me.
My heart does long for your strong arms to hold
Me once more, to float in love's fervent sea.
How cruel is Autumn with fruit laden,
Recalling times when we together grew.
As evening comes and daylight is fading,
My soul cries out, 'My love, I'm missing you.'
How like the Winter is your absence now
So cold, so bleak when heavy clouds hang low.

'Tis death has torn our two sweet lives apart.
Life is but sorrow now, nothing pleasing.
My grief has stripped the music from my heart;
Now clangs an empty gong, not appeasing.
You dwell in a new world beyond the skies,
Your flame is spent; in me what's left is rage.
But I must sing of you and those kind eyes,
For we will meet in yet a future age.
I must not grieve, my love, for we have been
Bound to each heart with cords eternal while
Traversing the long years both fat and lean.
I must learn how to dry my tears and smile.
After cold darkness does new light appear?
Farewell, my heart's desire, I loved you dear.

Wendy A Nottingham

THE RED, RED ROSE

See, here in my hand, is the red rose you sent to me
Still drinking deep, of the morning dew.
Fresh from Love's garden, 'twas gathered in ecstasy
To bear a message to me, from you.

Loves flower of happiness, regal flower of love.
Supreme you stood where the south wind blows.
Threefold perfume, remembrance, happiness and love.
I've found them all, in the heart of a rose.

This sweet red rose will wither and decay
It's perfume and colour be gone
But the message it brought will live for aye
And its memories linger on.

And should some petals fall, I'll leave them there
Till all the rose has withered and decayed.
Then I'll gather them all with tender care
And pack away each memory neatly arrayed.

Then at each anniversary, I will live again
The day you sent the rose
Yes I will live again
The day you sent the rose.

Bertha Dale

AUTUMNAL

When late Summer fades into Autumn
And ripening hedgerow fruits are awesome.
Autumn lilies are in open glades,
With bright yellow bracken in the shade.
Shrilling of grasshoppers, in the air
Wasps and jam sandwiches are the fare.
And the rays of the sun warm the soil
While nests of black garden ants do toil.
Then they swarm in the air, where they mate
Wheat is combined for the harvest fete.

On water lilies, perch damsel flies
And charms of gold finches perch near by
Curlews probe the mud with their long beaks
Flicking pebbles beside meadowsweet.
In the fields tiny harvest mice hide
Among brambles, they breed and abide.
Skipper butterflies search for nectar
Around platinum lakes, what a spectre!
Pine trees stand against a moonlit sky
Ghostly shadows tell evening is nigh.

Ann Easton

SOUNDS OF LIFE

A young child crying in the street
The sound of quickly running feet
The constant drip from a water tap,
The rhythm of the sea with its gentle lap
The sounds from softly swaying trees
The murmur of the summer breeze
Stray dogs barking to one another
The meal time call of a seeking mother
The frantic beat of an April shower
The grandfather clock ticking away the hour
A husbands cheery greeting to his wife
For me these are the sounds of life.

Rosemary Platt Heaney

Controversial/Correct

'Make haste ere you perish, there's flooding forecast.'
The rescue launch is waiting, no engine or mast.
This escape route is free, so climb aboard this boat.
No matter how absurd, you'll be safe as you float.

Rules have been issued by the reigning king.
Disregarding God, or anything
Bow to the golden image, or lose your life
Let idol worship prevail and you'll be alright.

One day a ship carrying fishermen, were fishing beside the shore
They had cast the nets throughout the night, and many hours more.
A voice came echoing across the sea
'Try the other side of the boat, and scores of fish you'll see.'

Did you hear of the criminal released today?
Barabbas the murderer. No remorse displayed.
Jesus was beaten and tortured in Barabbas' place.
Sad and rejected by the noisy crowd. He was thoroughly disgraced.

Only a few incidents reported in God's book
Many more therein. Open the covers and look.
Creation, abuse, love stories, rape.
Spine-chilling episodes which make the reader gape.

Really spectacular are the facts about Christ
Who was willing to die. A sacrifice of innocent life,
To redeem the world's sinners, of whom I am one
I'm now a saved mortal, because I trust in God's Son.

Biblical statements, forecast correct
God the creator never makes mistakes.
'Tis wise to pay heed before the last minutes are here.
Do we accept genuine warning, or disregard personal fear?

Only in Christ is our existence wholly complete.
He's the embodiment of life, without whom there's a need.

I Rosie

THE HURT

He will dance on our coffins she'd wearily say
To her husband whose eyes would turn sadly away
When he'd see, not a child, but a man who'd become
So frustrated he couldn't believe that his son.

Was so angry - aggressive - explosive with rage,
Screaming out 'I want company - friends my own age.'
Whilst his mother tried desperately hard to explain
How they both understood his frustration and pain.

'You don't care!' he'd storm past her and up to his room
Where the blast of his music vibrated - then soon
He'd be lost in the world he escaped to whilst she
Was left numb with despair at the futility.

Of the vibrant young life she'd seen shattered and torn
Because some erring gene from the day he was born
Had decided his fate - left him lacking the scope
To fit into where everyone else was to cope.

He'd play tapes, watch the telly - buy simplistic things
Whilst a yearning for that which young company brings
Was there writhing within him - frustration un-quelled
For a freedom denied him, and now he'd rebelled.

But his mother remembered that sensitive boy
Who'd been gentle and loving, would give his best toy
To whoever had wanted it - trust was to him
Such a simple and instinctively natural thing.

And she didn't know how to resolve all the hurt
That he'd suffered inside, except try to divert
Such confused mixed emotions, frustration and pain
Into hoping that one day he'd trust them again.

Jo Lewis

RHYME AND RHYTHM

A poem that has rhythm and rhyme.
Yes, it's about time
the pendulum finally swung back.
Back on the right track.

Rhyme delivered in sing-song voice.
Please give that choice.
Like tapping our feet to rock and roll
or to slow soul.

Tap a rhythm out by hand
Now make no sound.
Repeat the rhythm in our head.
'No problem,' you said!

'How do we do that?' someone asked
Babies do that task.
Nature gave us rhyme and rhythm
We should stick with 'em.

Christine Brain

Travel Fever

There's a suitcase, quite a new one
Open on a chair,
There's a place name on a label,
One, I know not where.

There are clothes, quite neatly folded
Jockeying for space,
Waiting for decision making
As momentum gathers pace.

Yes, I'm off on Tuesday morning
By coach across the sea;
A journey long, all through the night
To visit Italy.

My first time ever to the south
For ten days in the sun;
I find it hard still to believe,
But Garda, here I come.

There's a suitcase, used to travel
Filled with hope and care;
Trousers, shirts and shaving tackle
On another chair.

There's a man whom I love dearly
Whose great idea was this;
For both of us to go away,
A chance I cannot miss.

So, on Tuesday, our two cases
And their owners too
Join forces on our first time
To adventures new.

Denis has been oft before,
Has served there in the war;
He told me of the happy days,
But, is ready for some more.

The passports and the travellers cheques
Are safely stowed away;
The sleeping and seasickness pills
May not see light of day.

Now, I must end this little ditty,
I've really got to choose;
The red dress or the blue one,
The sandals or the shoes?

L Munden

Wish You Were Here?

Do not sit by my warm corpse and weep,
Though it's true I'm dead, and not asleep.
Come dry your eyes, shed no more tears,
'Cos where I'm going, there aren't any fears.
First stop's at hell,
To see the angel who fell.
Then it's Ping-Pong in purgatory,
Rather a monotonous story.
Next, onto limbo, less said the better,
It's run by a miserable bloke in a sweater.
Time for a detour by paradise,
Become sick of chocolate, not nice!
Finally get to Heaven and reach for the bell,
Met by an angel, male or female? Can't tell.
It looks at me twice, before shaking it's head,
Next thing I know, I'm back in my bed.
You're standing there, that look on your face.
Oh, how I wish I could take your place!

Clare Anne Lewis

REGRETS

Of years long past we recollect the pain
Of fear, anxiety and grief
Of struggles battling, oft in vain
Surviving somehow, life-span brief
Of war and bombs and loved ones gone
With rationed food and far off men
Touching no more, for whom we long
Communication always just by pen
Among the death there dwelt the feel
The warmth of people's spirit near
This was the strength that was so real
Keeping us going as we shed a tear
Rebuilding ties - we went without
Others were first of some
That years brought change there was no doubt
We waited for our turn to come.
Now age sits on our
Greying heads and forces us to please
And poverty and aching leave us blue
Heart whispers gently, life will surely ease
But sadly know, this is no longer true.

Hilary Ingle

MY MEMORY

At this age of sixty plus, do brain cells go to seed?
For, I try so hard with urgency to achieve the words I need.
Words, words and names, they evade with such dreadful trial,
I peruse the dictionary A to Z, but they're lost for quite a while.

What has happened to the system, it is chaotic, in disgrace,
My brain to mouth activity is lost without a trace.
I'm scared, truly I am, what is the future's sign?
Will I become inarticulate with grey matter in decline?

Conversations seem useless, words said
with meanings wrong,
And yet it's strange that sentences come so easily in song!
My eloquence has vanished, I ponder where it's gone,
I used to talk so freely, nattering to everyone.

I feel my memory is threadbare, never again to mend,
For the words I speak are contrary to those that I intend.
I have resolved to stay with simple words, then hurtful friends will stop.
Malenting with rehality - oh' no!
Lamenting with hilarity, that I'm the original Mrs Maleprop.

Lucy Bloxham

My Opinion

Never does a thought arise in my mind
Without a question of how it will find
Room in all the day's routine and plans
And not be forgotten as also ran.

It must take its place with many others
Resting awhile until all foregather
And one is selected on occasion
To be heard in words as my opinion.

Your love for me dear shows in all you do
And you can see that there is mine for you.
In all the things that we can do together,
For each other, is to care forever.

Hugh Lincoln

RHYTHMIC MEETINGS

Meetings may be ordinary,
Sometimes extraordinary.
Agenda deliberated,
Written minutes circulated.
Matters which arise selected -
Gnawed, chewed upon and dissected.
Best way forward worked out clearly.
Weekly, monthly, sometimes yearly.

Revival meetings' preachers shout
'Hallelujah! Do come on out
You sinners to the mercy seat.
Repent and make your lives complete.'
Moody drew Victorians near
And Sankey's hymns they flocked to hear.
Billy Graham in later days
Travelled far to promote his praise.

Gospel meetings condemning wrong,
Bible stories sing-a-long;
Rocking bodies, happy faces,
Repetition of key phrases;
Rocking bodies, happy faces,
Coloured folk first set the paces;
Rocking bodies, happy faces,
Reaching out to many races.

Humans like to hold their meetings,
Starting off with mutual greetings,
Agreeing on a course of action -
Completion brings them satisfaction,
Resolving what to do and be
Helps them to keep life orderly.

E Joan Knight

Autumn Mist

Out of grey and silvered autumn mist
Emerge pale, sallow trees, raggedly clad;
Jewelled, yet stooping, adorned, yet despoiled
Are the plants, like old women, garish and sad.

Windows drip their steam in patterned lines;
Shy smoke criss-crosses gardens past their prime;
Late roses cringe and curl up from the damp
But emerald grass recalls spring's richest time.

Sensing the sun, reluctant shapes appear;
Dahlias and chrysanthemums peep through
Earth based cloudlets, like a rainbow's palette,
Their flaring colours muted by the dew.

Transfigured by its bath, earth greets the sun;
Spiders' webs try in vain to keep their pearls.
The sky washed also gently deepens blue.
Everywhere the mystery of mist unfurls.

Hope Bunton

FRIENDSHIP

To have a true friend, no words can express.
The happiness found makes you feel truly blest.
To confide and to share good news and bad.
Thankfully always there, makes you feel oh so glad.
A sounding board just someone to care.
To find someone special, is often so rare.
You trust their advice, and know they're not wrong.
Treasure your friend for their time and support.
An understanding so special can never be bought.

Anne Sackey

ANIMAL MAGIC

The chameleon - that creature -
Is forever changing colour!
It's characteristic feature
Is to turn from one to another.

This kaleidoscopic reptile
For his camouflage is renowned,
In a class above the rank and file
Of reptilia on the ground.

He is really quite a fellow -
A master at concealment,
He can change from brown to yellow
By just a twitch of pigment!

When he changes his position
He can turn as green as myrtle,
He's a genius, a magician
Worthy of the Magic Circle!

There's no limit to his wizardry,
His skill extraordinaire -
He can disappear mysteriously
And yet he is still there.

His tongue, eight inches long at least,
At a stretch - so it is reckoned -
Can catch him a very tasty feast
In a fraction of a second!

He can do so many clever tricks -
An artist in his own right,
A brilliant illusionist -
O he leads such a colourful life!

Joyce Atkinson

DOUGHNUT DILEMMA

Mum, who put the hole in this doughnut?
Why has the jam all escaped?
How is it Grandad can take out his teeth
And complain he can't stand chocolate cake?
And these calories you're always counting -
Well I cannot see them at all!
You must have a good eye
For in Gran's cherry pie
You can count eighteen hundred and four!
Mum, why must I eat all this lettuce
Tomatoes and coleslaw and ham?
Oh bring back the rest of my doughnut
'Cos I miss my strawberry jam!

Tony McLarty

Parallel Lines

Parallel lines =
never meeting, never greeting,
being apart . . . forever keeping.
Parallel lines =
not any nearer yet failing to be further,
a persistent distance, an equal constraint,
a sequel of restraint.
Parallel lines =
geometrically sound, possibly square,
maybe round. Vertical, horizontal, straight
or diagonal, a bending angle or an imaginary tangle.
Parallel lines =
a dual disposition out of the dimension,
a distant destination for the duration
and a direct deliverance into the distance.
Parallel lines =
nothing definite, everything infinite,
preparing to wait, caring to anticipate,
never too early, ever so late.

Simon King

SEASONS

The buds are forming on the trees
Young shoots are peeping through the ground
A gentle humming of the bees
And butterflies that make no sound.

They dart about from flower to flower
Their colours dazzling in the sun
The clouds roll up to bring a shower
And the air smells fresh since the rain has come.

Young lambs are frolicking in the fields
The foal is wobbly on his legs
You can hear the piglets squeals
And the farmer's careful where he treads.

How hot and humid the days are now
The animals look for some shaded tree
Which now have leaves on every bough
Making it cool for you and me.

A storm is brewing, the sky is dark
Umbrellas up and hurry home
Children scatter from the park
Which looks forlorn and all alone.

Where are all the colours now?
The leaves are changing on the trees
shades of red, yellow and brown
Nights turn cold and it starts to freeze.

Winter has arrived at last
The trees so bare now covered in snow
A carpet of white which looks so vast
Small birds imprints begin to show.

All nature has a part to play
In the beauty we see day by day.

Y Corcoran

BUZZING OFF

The air holds now the nip of autumn chill,
Those that of nectar drink are getting tired,
Searching for the flowers that linger still,
Which are by bees so ardently desired.

The summer plants the white faced bindweed finds,
Takes grasses, blooms and leaves within it's grip,
Tenacious vine that winds and twists and climbs,
Holds the plant tight so creatures cannot sip.

Impeding that fast flowing energy,
Sucked freely from each open hearted bloom,
The plants are sealed from buzzing wasp and bee,
As bindweed cups like sepulchres entomb.

The people's lily blooms so far and wide,
It's goblets soft hold poison in their white,
A pale reaper who will not be denied,
A cobra like constricting parasite.

The autumn leaves like fires of gold and red,
One last bright burnished gleam before they fall,
Burned by the sun who once those young leaves fed,
The harvest time is here for one and all.

Then when the winter covers everything,
Some may retreat to under surface dark,
But spring's return is worth remembering,
Like poppies of remembrance in the park.

Kathleen M Scatchard

SUNSET

Its last rays glistening gently on the sea,
The sun slips, like a ball of fire, from sight;
The sky that was so blue turns slowly red
And on the water sheds a rosy light.
So ends another perfect summer day
As sunset heralds the approaching night.

Small waves dance lightly on the golden sand,
A-ripple like arpeggios back and fore;
The ebbing tide leaves shallow pools behind,
With shells and seaweed scattered on the shore.
Soft, softer grows the music of the sea,
A slow diminuendo, then no more.

The night is tranquil - just a fleeting breath
Exudes a Presence tangible and sweet,
That rests like gossamer upon the soul
And bids it come to worship at his feet;
For those who wish to hear the stillness speaks,
In harmony man and his maker meet.

Barbara Jones

A SECOND HEAVEN

Flowers yellow and flowers red,
Each a floral delight in a flower bed,
Flowers pink and flowers blue,
A complex array of colours and hue,
Flowers short and flowers tall,
Flowers big and flowers small,
Flowers grown in the greenhouse there,
Lovingly planted and nurtured with care.
Now they dance in the gentle breeze
That filters through the well-pruned trees.
Trees and shrubs and bushes too,
Climbers' arches to walk through.
Turf immaculately laid,
Lawns of perfection made.
Crazy paved paths and paths of gravel,
Obscure walkways to unravel.
Before the summerhouse a garden pool
Where goldfish dart in water cool.
A place where birds upon the wing
Alight on bough to rest and sing.
A place where butterflies in colours gay
Flutter as fallen petals all the day.
A place where bees their business pursue
Ever industrious, forever true.
A place where all may sit in style
To rest their weary legs awhile.
If God on Earth a second Heaven make,
Please - in a garden - for Heaven's sake.

Percy Walton

CHILDHOOD DAYS

Reminiscing on days long past,
When we were very small,
Long summer nights, trips on the tram,
Are memories I recall.
Taking my sisters to the local park,
Of course my brothers came too.
Picnic packed in Mam's shopping bag,
Tea in the pot to brew.
Life seemed to be less hectic,
Things moved at a slower pace,
No telly to watch, no computers,
And videos . . . not a trace.
Our house was a four-roomed terrace,
No garden, only a yard,
No bathroom, no central heating
Wasn't life hard!
We even shared our bedrooms,
The boys with Mam and Dad,
The girls slept in the back room,
It really wasn't so bad.
Despite our many problems,
We were always very glad
That we belonged to a family,
And our childhood wasn't sad.
We are all now much older,
Have gone our different ways,
Sadly one brother is missing
From our childhood days.
We still share time together or telephone,
Recalling days long past, when we lived at home.

Betty Kirkham

A SCOTSMAN FROM TROON

There once was a Scotsman from Troon
Who decided to fly to the moon
He thought it was time to create a sensation!
And act on behalf of his proud little nation
to fulfil his ambition, to accomplish his dream
He would build a spacecraft that was his scheme
With bits of scrap metal, an old window, and door
And an engine so heavy it buckled the floor
Soon, the time came, the launch day was here
Friends from miles around turned up to cheer
The take-off, no more than a horrible sound
When the dust settled he was still on the ground
Stepping from the wreck of his backyard creation
Thinking he had made it, he was filled with elation!
Till he heard a voice, a familiar sound in his life
Of course it was none other, than his partner, his wife.

Karl Jakobsen

ADAM AND EVE

When God created woman
of a rib from Adam's side
He said 'Go forth and multiply
for she will be your bride'

Old Adam thought his luck was in
to be given such a prize
But Adam who had never sinned
was soon to realise

This woman who was fair of face
and a beauty to behold
Was just as cunning as the snake
and sometimes just as cold.

For Eve 'that's what God named her'
knew how to get her way
She also knew right from the start
just how to make man pay

And Adam was besotted
he thought she was the cream
But he learned from his misfortune
things aren't always what they seem

For Eve was a seductress
a temptress and a flirt
So devious were her methods
poor Adam she did hurt

One day she said to Adam
'Let us eat the fruit of sin'
And although he was reluctant
he very soon gave in

Then God did visit Adam
and told him in disgrace
'You are supposed to be a man
so put her in her place'

So from that moment on
the battle did begin
The fight between the sexes
that nobody can win.

Pauline Tattersall

When I Am Gone

When I am gone, weep not for me.
Praise give one other - yet to be,
Who stands by you. Then in a while
The flicker of a gentle smile
Will light your face for all to see.

Remembering the things that we
Enjoyed in youth - hilariously.
Do not let sorrow cramp your style
When I am gone.

To earn my immortality
I need to know that you agree
Our love was true - devoid of guile.
Let others take their place in file.
This bond will keep you close to me
When I am gone.

Lena Cooper

THE MAY TREE

Covered in blossoms of pink and white,
Serene as a bride, a glorious sight.
Every bough adorned with a fragrant flower,
This pretty may tree makes a lovely bower.
Alas such beauty is short and sweet,
When strong winds and rain on her blossoms beat,
And plucked like confetti from her branches it floats,
Down to the ground and lies a beautiful coat,
Of pink and white petals, oh what a shame,
For the beautiful May tree and her short lived fame.

Rita M Arksey

ODE TO A LOLLIPOP

How do I love thee, lollipop?
In a sherbet dab that fizzes on the tongue,
Sucking slowly, lasting long.
Raspberry coated cool ice-cream,
Fruity candy, pink or green.
Chewy toffee on a stick,
Not too many you'll be sick.

Big and red beside the road,
While children learn the green cross code,
Reminding me of childhood days
When life was sweet in many ways.
Not governed by the broom and mop
But by pennies taken to the shop
To buy a luscious lollipop.

Joyce Walker

HAPPINESS

'I am happy' is a scarcely used phrase
People claim to be on top of the world
Not knowing whether it's real or a craze
Humans eager to flash teeth nicely pearled.

Happiness is fleeting it comes and goes
Like death or a shadow you never know
When it may spring upon you like a rose
Or when it will fade and make you so low.

We all yearn for happiness it's a drug
Yet we don't realise it when it's there
Are we happy in love locked in a hug?
Or is it when we have not a care.

Happiness is personal, embrace it
And your face will be glowing, brightly lit.

Natasha Raheem

HARD TIMES

I am skint, I am broke,
This is getting beyond a joke.
Wish I had a bob or two,
Just to help me see the week through.
I don't know, what can I say,
All the flaming bills to pay.
I've pawned me granny, me grandad too,
Just what the heck am I to do?
I ain't got tuppence, not even a cent,
At least, thank God, I've paid the rent!
Unemployable, can't get a job,
Just because I'm a lazy slob.
It's not right, it's just not fair,
Why can't I be a millionaire?
Live in a mansion and own a yacht,
Instead just look at what I've got.
A clapped out banger, a wreck of a thing,
Held together with glue and bits of string.
A seedy flat on a council estate,
And Buckingham Palace, it sure ain't.
This is driving me up the wall,
Robbing Peter just to pay Paul.
Sometimes I think I'd be better off dead,
But lend me a tenner, till Wednesday instead!

Doreen Morfitt

REPARTEE IN RHYME

The rock of Gibraltar wasn't always British,
At one time General De Gaulle did own.
But it wasn't always known as the rock of Gibraltar,
It was known as De Gaulle Stone.

My wife watches most soaps,
But so does her mum.
The programmes include Emeriod Farm and Constipation Street,
And they are definitely a pain in the bum.

I said to my wife 'Would you like a drink?'
And my wife replied 'Oh yes, I would love a cup of tea.'
I then said 'Oh good dear, while you are making one for yourself,
Will you make one for me?'

Did you know that the first sign of madness is hair in the palms
                                        of your hands?
And that they can be your downfall and ruin,
And the second sign is looking for them,
Which is now what you are doing.

John P Evans

DADDY, I DON'T LIKE BEING LOST

The family their journey had started after darkness fell,
But a vital turn was missed somehow, though where none could tell,
And, to their destination, suddenly the way was unclear,
With those must wanted road signs failing strangely to appear,
Till, in just six little words, their daughter's unease came across,
As 'Daddy' she said simply, 'I don't like being lost.'

And here in this child's words, expressing her concern
Is a much deeper truth God would have all to learn,
For, looking down from heaven, the Father on high
Longs, from every heart, to hear a similar cry,
In recognition of their true spiritual state,
As their desperate need of Him each would appreciate.

For, unwilling that even one soul should be lost
God gave His very best, at immeasurable cost -
The darling of His bosom, the Lord Jesus Christ,
Who would die in our place, to pay sin's bitter price,
And bring the direction and purpose our lives lacked before,
Opening the door for us also to life evermore.

Yes, His mission to the lost was to seek and to save,
With seeming defeat turned to victory at the empty grave,
For, having borne our punishment on Calvary's cursed tree,
The now triumphant, risen Saviour can set bound sinners free,
And through His Spirit, the Bible, and precious times on our knees
He can steer, guide and direct through life's perplexities.

And, preparing now a place, where streets with gold are paved,
It is Jesus' earnest wish that all would be saved,
For the arms of His welcome and mercy exclude none,
And to the very ends of the earth His invitation is 'Come' -
Life abundant and eternal is freely offered today
To all who trust Christ as Saviour - the Truth, Life and Way.

Ian Caughey

THE GOLDEN LINK

A golden bracelet when she was two,
'Look' I said, 'It's just for you!'
Wear it always every day,
When you are eating, asleep or at play,
A golden link from me to you,
Tied with satin bows of blue.

'This is for you,' her young man sighed,
As he gave the gold chain to his bride,
'Wear it my love and think of me,
When I am gone, and away at sea.
A golden link to show our love,
Joined together by God above.'

On our Golden wedding our children three,
Gave us both a golden key.
'It's the key of our hearts,' they said with a smile,
'For you have reached a golden mile.
Joined together with golden ring,
A link to the joys we're remembering.'

Memories will not fade away,
The joys stay with us every day,
And I thank God both day and night,
For giving us this golden light.
It shines on us in sun and rain,
Our golden link may God sustain.

Peggy Briston

BALLAD OF THE DALES WAY

Aire, Litton, Nid, Swale, Ure and Wharfe,
A formidable array -
On muddy footpath, steep incline,
We tread the Dales Way.

Meadowsweet, Cranesbill, garlic wild.
Sweet Cicely today
Fills our nostrils as we go
Along the Dales Way.

Wensleydale cheese and Thixton beer
To keep the wolf at bay -
There's always a cosy pub somewhere
Along the Dales Way.

Fresh falling shower, slanting rain,
Hail, snow, the sun's sharp ray -
Refreshed, we face the elements
Along the Dales Way.

The rivers wind and never rest.
We may decide to stay
In Grassington, Hawes or Muker,
All on the Dales Way.

Shadows of grasses dance in the wind,
Reeds in the water sway
And each new morning we step out
Along the Dales Way.

Please to close the five-barred gate
Lest the sheep should stray.
Shallows dip and whirl as they please
Over the Dales Way.

Every season brings delight -
Hoar frost, sweet-smelling hay,
Lambs, snowdrops, crisp leaves crunching
Underfoot on the Dales Way.

Grey churches nestle in the dale.
Though now we seldom pray
In them, I think there's plenty of praise
About on the Dales Way.

Here's to the English countryside,
That long its beauty may
Sustain our sometimes flagging steps
Along the Dales Way.

Jacqueline Abendstern

LAMENT FOR A LOST AGE

Over clustered rooftops to distant country steeples
Town dwellers gaze and think of country people,
Toiling hard on farm estates,
Thinking to themselves, 'How great,
To breathe air free from smog and dust,'
Not thinking of the ancient plough that rusts.
Redundant in a super-age where 'combines' rule,
They've done away with things that used to break your back.
No longer do they tread the track
With scythes and flagons full of ale -
Every second's up for sale.
Yes, all is up for sacrifice
If it is seen to have a price:
To get the job much quicker done
Is now what urges things along.
No time to sit and rest the plough -
All's different in the country now.

John Eastaugh

WESTERN HERO

Riding out across the sand dunes, down towards the sea,
A cowboy and his partner, waved hello to me,
He had a smile upon his face, my heart it skipped a beat,
Who knows, maybe one day, we may even meet.

My horse was getting very tired, it was time to head for town,
We turned and headed inland, as the rain came falling down,
I don't know what happened, I only know I took a fall,
So I lay in the sand dunes, trying hard to call.

Everything kept going dark, my eyes they could not see,
But suddenly I could feel, someone close to me,
He lifted me upon his horse, and headed into town,
Riding through the darkness, the rain still falling down.

The cowboy that had saved me, was the one who waved hello,
He really is the best man, I will ever know,
Now when Marshall Jay Dee, comes on into town,
I know that he will be with me, when the sun goes down.

Lesley Allen

JUST A DAY

My eyes scan the heavens in the morning light,
   transient clouds 'cross heaven drift,
a translucent sky replaces the night
   and the sun greets the Earth in a lover's tryst.

When midday comes, a deeper blue,
   noonday heat and shimmering air.
In late afternoon an azure hue,
   the pink in the evening means tomorrow is fair.

My eyes see the stars at the close of the day,
   a million beacons to light the night sky.
I can see all their wonder from the ground where I lay,
   my eyes scan the heavens, I see the clouds floating by.

Colin Spicer

LUMBERJACK LOP, HIS BALLAD

Lumberjack Lop gave a good chop
  He had spent years and years
Giving a good crop.
  Accidentally one fine day,
Poor Lumberjack Lop forgot to stop.
  The tree bent backwards in a strop,
For the first time in years and years
  He was a flop.
Poor Lumberjack Lop he didn't 'alf drop.

B I Grime

PURDY - RESCUE CAT

When first I saw her I thought - what's that?
An ugly, black, moth-eaten cat.
And then I looked again and saw a range
Of colours, blended rich and strange,
Black and gold and grey and tabby,
With fur all dull and rough and shabby.
One torn ear and a peculiar nose
With a distinctive touch of permanent rose.
I looked again in front and saw
One mayo and one cocoa paw!
But then I thought - I'll take a chance,
Perhaps with TLC she might advance.
At home poor dog Tina took one look
And screamed so high the rafters shook.
The cat ignored her
And I implored her to be quiet.
As I considered the cost of feline diet.
Now four years later I have a purring friend
Upon whose presence I can depend.
She's never been a lap cat -
Oh no, not that.
And her fur's still barred gold, black and tabby,
But now it's silken soft and far from shabby.
Her curious nose
Has kept its touch of permanent rose,
But I've got used to it now and I wouldn't change
An inch of her wonderful, colourful patchwork range.

Eileen M Lodge

SYMBIOSIS

Unleash the address to her eyes,
As I spy her across the room,
So that I may impress and surprise,
And release her from her doom,
So that I may make a career,
From her convalescent heart,
I'll promise there's no fear,
Of it being torn apart,
I'll ask her to dance,
And break the ice,
And take a chance,
And roll the dice,
And if my number is her call,
And I'm in fashion with her soul,
Then she will take me as her lover,
For I believe we are each other.

Anthony John Ward

SHIMMERING

(For Tony - 'Chhota Bhai'!)

'Let nothing disturb thee,
Nothing afright . . .'
God of the sea-sheen
Brighten thy night!

Though thy frail craft be storm-tossed,
And far from dry land,
The God of white waters
Hold thee safe in his hand!

May he pilot thy boat with thee,
Unseen, but bright;
Lord of the journey-home,
And the riding-light.

Eileen Pennell

(* Chhota Bhai' - Hindustani for 'Little Brother')

THE ROBIN AND THE PANDA

(Or how Robin got his red breast and Panda his black eyes)

The panda - deep inside the woods, was wandering aimlessly
When he heard a friendly chirrup, high above him in a tree
Where on a branch - there sat a bird - with chest of crimson red
'How did you get that lovely hue,' the black and white panda said
'I'm not sure how it happened, but I'm given to understand
I got this blood red chest, the time I perched upon the hand
Of a man - who slowly dying - was nailed onto a tree
For there upon a wooden cross, He suffered agony
Then as I flew to comfort Him - His mark was left on me
A staining of His dying blood - for all mankind to see
He gave His life so all the world from sin could be set free
They say He was a saviour - He was God's only son
Nails pierced his feet - thorns tore His head, for love of ev'ryone
He hung alone upon that cross - battered, bruised and weak -
Not for himself - but sinners - the tears coursed down His cheek
I wanted to be near Him, as His friends and Mother cried
As He said 'Father forgive them' then loving us He died'
The panda inconsolable - as the story reached his ears
Put big black paws up to his eyes, to wipe away the tears
'I wish I could be like you - and bear a sign' he said
'Of the man - who for the love of us - hung on that cross and bled'
'I'm afraid I have to go now' Robin said and flew away
While the panda bears the paw marks round his eyes unto this day.

Irene Beattie

'HOUSE LIGHTS'

When the Overture's calling
And you feel that you're falling
Into bottomless space
With the thrill of the race
It's 'stage kisses' that
Don't mean a thing
And 'stage whispers'
That mean everything
The curtain is up
And you're on!

Bryn Bartlett

BUTTERFLY IN SILENCE CAME

Butterfly in silence came,
Without a whisper of your name.
Fluttering on the summer wind,
Come to me and gently sing.

O butterfly, passing by
Silhouette against the sky.
Performing on this open stage,
Perform for me as I laze.

Settle on a vacant flower,
Still like the departing hour.
Delicate as silver webs,
Hung with dew as twilight ebbs.

Fleeting moments you instil,
Pulsating wings answering a will.
Traveller of stray sunbeams,
Stay, linger in my sultry dreams.

Colin Farmer

ME

As I stand upon the shore
Gazing at the mighty sea
I wonder what life has in store
What does the future hold for me

Will I be a sailor braving that sea
Sailing away and feeling so free
Or will my life be on the shore
With my talents, if any, to the fore

Will I be a writer or maybe a singer
An orchestra leader, perhaps a bell ringer
A leader of men on a field of sport
Even a doctor now there's a thought

Will I be an actor or a politician
I really don't know that maybe just wishing
So many things for which to strive
I'm just thankful I'm alive

There are lots of things that I could be
But all I am is young and free
And when all is said and done you see
I'm just glad that I am me.

Donald Linnett

TRAVELLER'S SONNET

(Dedicated to Dr Gary Shaw GP)

I am going, I will not stay awhile,
The journey's walk I take is hard and long,
I'll think of you in every traveller's mile,
And love that's past will kindle new love strong.
Yet if I forget your enchanting face,
Amid the turmoil of my lonely quest,
It is that which I seek beyond this race,
That drives away all thought of you and rest.
So may there be no pain in our parting,
But in fondest absence, consummation
Of true love, that mind's union of loving
Adoration, born from heart's searchings won,
Thus love being so though divided not,
By the journey is then true love begot.

Barry Bradshaw